Green With Envy

Written by Terri Sabol   Illustrated by Pei Jen

Blade is a light green blade of grass. His cousin, Augustine, is a dark green blade of grass on the opposite side of the yard...

The good side. The greener side. Augustine always gets the best of everything...

The best weather...

The best location...

The best view...

Blade is green with envy, but not as green as Augustine.

Blade thinks At least we both get a little taken off the top every Saturday. Though Augustine is always first in line for her haircut.

Blade is tired of
missing out.

I'm not going to stand for this any longer.

When the sun travels across the sky, Blade leans to the right, he leans to the left, and the shadows still cover him all day.

But Blade isn't giving up.

The next time the sprinklers come on, Blade stretches, he reaches, and he still comes up short.

But Blade isn't giving up.

When the kids come out to play, Blade hollers, he waves, and he still gets passed over.

But Blade isn't giving up.

Augustine is in the middle of the action when the family plays with Dog.

"Great catch, Dog!"

Blade whistles and calls, but he is overlooked.

"Here, Doggy!"

Blade wilts and sinks into the earth,
ready to give up on his green dream.

Why shouldn't I pursue my goal of living the high life?

One windy day, Blade decides to uproot himself and goes the whole nine yards across the lawn. He plants himself next to Augustine.

"Hey Blade! What are you doing on my turf?"

"Augustine, you shouldn't be the only one having all the fun."

Blade rakes it all in.

He's first for a haircut,

soaks up the sun,

drinks more water than
ever before,

squeals
watching the
kids play,

and roots for Dog
playing catch.

"This is the life!"

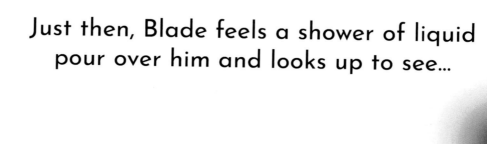

Just then, Blade feels a shower of liquid
pour over him and looks up to see...

"On second thought, I like my old home better.
See you later, Augustine!"

I guess I know why the grass is greener!

To my parents, who always taught me to appreciate what I have and to work hard for what I want. - T.S.

To my family members, who always encourage and support me. --P.J.

For information regarding permission, write to

Burning the Midnight Oil Publishing
1860 FM 359 #173, Richmond, TX 77406 USA.

ISBN: 978-1-946428-13-4
Library of Congress Control Number: 2020910282

Book Design and Cover by Pei Jen
Author Photograph by Sam Schultze

With many thanks to: Candice Hazlett Jensen, Leslie Helakoski, and Karen Syblik for their support and encouragement.

Made in the USA
Middletown, DE
06 August 2020